MATCHBOX TOYS

1982 Limited Edition Pack of 5 Models

"BP"
2603
BRITISH PETROLEUM
COMPANY LTD. 12MPH

CHIVERS
&
SONS LTD

Jams, Jellies, & Marmalades
THE ORCHARD FACTORY
HISTON
CAMBRIDGE

'MATCHBOX'

models of
yesteryear®

BIRD'S
CUSTARD POWDER
MAKES THE RICHEST CUSTARD WITHOUT EGGS
AT HALF THE COST & TROUBLE
THE ORIGINAL & ONLY GENUINE
Alfred Bird & Sons,
BIRMINGHAM.

EVANS
BROS. COAL & COKE

8+YEARS. CONTAINS FIVE MODELS. 8+ANS. CONTIENT CINQ MODELES. 8+JAHRE. INHALT FÜNF MODELL.

MATCHBOX TOYS

A Quantum Book

Published by Grange Books
an imprint of Grange Books Plc
The Grange
Kingsnorth Industrial Estate
Hoo, nr Rochester
Kent ME3 9ND

ISBN 1 84013 277 9

This book is produced by
Quantum Books Ltd
6 Blundell Street
London N7 9BH

Project Manager: Rebecca Kingsley
Art Director: Siân Keogh
Project Editor: Jo Wells
Designer: Martin Laurie
Assistant Designer: Sandra Marques
Editor: Kay Macmullan

The material in this publication previously appeared in *Matchbox Toys*

QUMCCMT
Set in Gill Sans
Reproduced in Singapore by Eray Scan Pte Ltd
Printed in Singapore by Star Standard Industries (Pte) Ltd

CONTENTS

HOW MATCHBOX BEGAN

• • • •

BELOW Jack Odell and Leslie Smith at the height of their success in the mid-Sixties.

After World War II two school friends, Leslie Smith and Rodney Smith, would meet again, return to their pre-war jobs and follow through on a schoolboy pact they had made to start a company together.

The two Smiths had lost touch before the war, but when they were both sent to the same Royal Naval base to be demobilized, they once more talked about their dreams of founding an engineering firm.

Before the war, Leslie Smith had worked for a London confirming house that specialized in shipping items to Australia, New Zealand, and the Far East. Rodney, not related to Leslie, returned to his job with a die-casting firm. Occasionally, they would meet and plan for their futures. Ultimately, they decided they would pool their talents – Leslie in sales and Rodney in die-casting – and form the company they had dreamed about. In January, 1947, Lesney Products was founded, the name combining the first syllable of Leslie and the last syllable of Rodney.

Starting up

Working capital was the first challenge for the new company, which bought its first die-casting machine from Rodney's old employer. The next problem was to find a workplace. They located a rundown pub in North London and the machine on which they had staked their future, was positioned where the bar had been.

LEFT A Lesney
factory at
Hackney, London
– a far cry from
the pub where the
company started.

A new partner

At the same time, John William Odell, known as Jack, who had worked for Rodney's ex-firm was also looking to set up on his own. He purchased some war surplus equipment including lathes, millers and grinders, and figured he would set up his business in his mother's garage. When he was told that the garage could not be used for industrial purposes he approached Rodney Smith to ask if he could store his machinery with him.

A deal was made and so began one of the most productive and creative alliances in toy-making history.

Odell set about designing his own products and as the three men worked under the same roof, Jack's skill soon became apparent. He was enlisted to make the dies for Lesney Products and eventually became a full partner in the firm.

By late 1947, Lesney was getting enough work to keep eight men busy and possessed more than 30 moulds and dies.

BELOW The
Aveling Barford
Road Roller – the
first of the
economy models.

7

Scale Model MILK CART MADE IN ENGLAND

ABOVE The milk cart was the first model to appear in its own individual box.

first in the line, was not boxed. Instead, a tray holding a dozen was taken around the local shops.

Dinky's marketing system, limiting its products to exclusive toy shops, and selling directly to the public, helped Matchbox gain access to new markets. Shopkeepers who couldn't stock Dinky toys were delighted to have something similar to sell.

The Kohnstam link

In 1947 to 1948, Richard Kohnstam of J. Kohnstam & Co emerged on the Lesney scene. Under the 'Moko' trademark, Kohnstam sold toys made by other toymakers and by 1894 the company had assembled a huge array of toys that were sold across Europe.

Established in Britain since 1890, at the outbreak of World War I the firm of M. Kohnstam & Co was requisitioned. Son Julius, however, in 1912 had set up a doll-making workshop in London. When the war ceased in 1918, Julius was ready to take up where he had ended with a toy business. Later, in 1923, Julius also

Making toys

The end of the year was a quiet time, so when a toy manufacturer asked Lesney to make a capgun part, they were quick to take on the order. Some employees also asked if they could make toys for their children at this time. Permission was granted, with the understanding that the toys be sold to shops too.

By studying the products of Dinky toys, the partners of Lesney came up with a line of 'economy models': a Diesel Road Roller, a Cement Mixer, a Caterpillar/Crawler Tractor, and a Caterpillar/Crawler Bulldozer. The Aveling Barford Diesel Road Roller, the

BELOW The Prime Mover, Trailer and Bulldozer came complete with loading ramps, and removable panels on the engine compartment – for 'repairs'.

incorporated a business to market tin-plated clockwork toys. Several items sold by this new company bore the old 'Moko' label. In 1933 Julius formed the company Dollies Ltd and the following year brother Emil joined Julius and became the head of the new company.

Julius died in 1935, leaving his brother Emil and son Richard to take care of the family's toy operations. In 1939 Richard went off to war while his uncle remained with the companies. At the end of the war Richard and Emil continued the business of selling and distributing die-cast toys and made 'Moko' their registered trademark in 1949.

Moving on

In March 1949 Lesney became incorporated as a private company. The quarters at *The Rifleman* were replaced by newer facilities in the East End of London.

The two Smiths and Odell were eager to bring out more toys a bit larger than the line that would be developed and known as Matchbox Kingsize. These

included a horse-drawn milk cart, a horse-drawn rag-and-bone cart, and a soapbox racer. The Prime Mover, Trailer and Bulldozer was issued in 1950 and was the largest of the early toys.

Zinc ban

Plans were also set for creating a large casting of the Royal State Coach. With the beginning of the Korean War, zinc (an ingredient of the mazac metal used for the die-cast toys) was banned for use in anything but vital products. Although Lesney had stockpiled considerable supplies of zinc, the ban meant harsh times for the company. The first casualty of the zinc ruling was the large State Coach.

Most of Lesney's other work had been dropped in favour of its line of toys. Fearing the demise of Lesney, Rodney Smith decided to leave. Meanwhile, Lesney

ABOVE The miniature coronation coach helped to trigger the Match 1–75 miniature series. These were fragile models, however, and few have survived.

RIGHT The 1–75 series Aveling Barford Road Roller No 1 differed from the earlier Lesney equivalent in that it had a driver.

needed something to help to weather the ban, so Odell secured a contract for making castings in car production.

At the end of the zinc ban, and with the coronation of Queen Elizabeth II in 1953, the time was right for the issue of the large Royal State Coach. A problem had arisen though. The coach was originally designed to show the late King and his Queen inside it. The decision was made not to modify the coach because it was assumed that Prince Philip would ride with the new Queen and the two figures would still be appropriate. Just over one hundred of the coaches were made when it was announced that Her Majesty would ride alone. Very quickly, the male figure was machined out of the mould. Ultimately, over 33,000 State Coaches were made and sold.

ABOVE: Jack Odell discovered the Norvic Matchbox that would contain the new miniature toys. Matchbox used a very similar design for their own boxes.

Also, with the end of the zinc ban, Lesney produced Muffin the Mule, an animal character from a popular BBC children's show, for Moko.

Odell then created a miniature of the Royal State Coach, of which more than one million would eventually be produced.

Matchbox

Matchbox was born when Odell created a miniature road roller made from brass that fitted snugly into the matchbox that his older daughter took to school to hold her toy. When Jack was swamped with requests to make additional road rollers, he decided to make a mould for casting copies of the toy. The initial outlay was about £100 and enabled him to make as many copies as he needed. He also discovered a matchbox from the Norvic Match Co Ltd of Czechoslovakia which contained the new toy perfectly.

1–75 Series

The Aveling Barford Road Roller (No 1), the Muir Hill Site Dumper (No 2), the Cement Mixer (No 3) and the Massey Harris Tractor (No 4), all scaled down from the earlier and larger Christmas toys, were the first miniatures in the new 1–75 series.

Made in 1953, they were packaged in yellow and blue small boxes and bore the lines 'Matchbox Series' and 'A Moko Lesney Product'. The number of the issued toy was also printed on each box.

After a slow start, sales started picking up, particularly after the introduction of the London double-decker bus (No 5).

Soon, new issues followed: the Quarry Truck (No 6), the Horse-drawn Milk Float (No 7), the Caterpillar Tractor (No 8), and the Dennis Fire Engine (No 9).

Problems arose for Leslie and Jack when they discovered that Richard Kohnstam had already registered the trademark 'Matchbox'. Leslie Smith and Odell decided that the name 'Moko' would not appear on any of the toys themselves. But for the moment, Kohnstam was entitled to market the new toys at home and in Europe, as well as a few other locations.

So Smith, who had important contacts throughout the world from his previous sales job, turned his attention to other markets where Moko was not in the way, particularly the United States, New Zealand and Australia.

New markets

At first, there were several importers recruited for the United States market, but the Fred Bronner Corporation became the sole importer in 1956. Another of Jack Odell's ideas, the Models of Yesteryear series was unveiled in 1956. Although Leslie Smith originally opposed the new line and its name, the success of the idea has a 36–year history.

BELOW The miniature horse-drawn milk float, shown here with its Lesney equivalent, was the only horse-drawn model in the 1–75 series.

NUMBERING SYSTEMS

Up until 1982 the numbered identification system was fairly straightforward. Within the 1–75 miniature series, each new model was given a number, from 1 to 75, and a letter, to indicate its place in the models of that number.

Within various numbers and letters, however, the colour and detail on models were often changed. These altered models could be introduced as a new model and assigned a new letter within the model's number; sometimes, they were given a new number and a new letter. Often, however, the number and letter were kept the same and the change was listed as a 'variation'.

ABOVE The box illustration shows the correct colouring for the wreck truck. Here is one of the very few models that were painted incorrectly.

Number – letter – number

As collectors needed a way to identify a model's place within the line-up and also its colour and other variations a 'number-letter-number' system was introduced whereby the number and letter were determined by the range and its sequence within that range and the various colour differences were noted by including a number after the letter.

Numbering a problem

Any stability within the numbering system began to fall apart in 1981 as the system was changed to produce different lines for the United States and the rest of the world (ROW).

Some models – the 'core' line-up – were common to both the US and the ROW and even used the same number but a few appear in both series but use different numbers. Various models appear in one range but not in the other and, occasionally, a model that would prove popular in the one range would suddenly be issued in the other range under the same or a different number.

In 1982, the model numbers disappeared from the undersides of the vehicles: putting numbers on them was leading to problems even for Matchbox itself.

Models of Yesteryear

The Models of Yesteryear range is numbered in a different way again. Each model is given a number but then numbers are also used to designate the position that the model holds within that number. For example, Y1–1 is the Allchin Traction Engine issued in 1956; Y1–2, a 1911 Model T Ford (1964); and Y1–3, a 1936 SS100 Jaguar (1977).

Issues of a current model in new liveries do not result in a renumbering of any sort. Occasionally, one might see the models from the Yesteryear line listed in a 'number-letter' system whereby a Y-1A would be the equivalent of a Y1–1. (Beginning with the 1988 catalogue, Matchbox changed the 'T' Yesteryear prefix to 'YY'.)

Skybusters

Skybusters are generally numbered according to the type of aircraft that they represent. An SB10 is a Boeing 747. Changes in the aeroplanes' livery are not recorded as new models.

Occasionally, when two liveries are available concurrently for the same model, the distinctions are differentiated with a letter added to the number. The SB23, a Concorde, is available in both the British Airways livery (SB23A) and the Air France livery (SB23B).

RIGHT A number of models within the Skybusters range are shown together on this shop display unit. The NASA Space Shuttle, on the top, was introduced as an SB3, replacing the A300 Airbus.

No 1	Allchin Steam Engine	59¢	No 4	Steam Lorry	59¢	No 7	4 Ton Leyland Truck	59¢
No 2	Double Decker Bus	59¢	No 5	Le Mans Bentley 1929	59¢	No 8	1926 Morris Cowley	59¢
No 3	Double Decker Tram Car	59¢	No 6	World War I Lorry	59¢	No 9	Showman's Engine	98¢

Kohnstam out

In 1956 Leslie Smith threatened to remove the names 'Matchbox' and 'Moko' from all connections with the toys simply by throwing away the boxes. Kohnstam agreed to re-register the name 'Matchbox' to Lesney and Moko

Lesney finally bought Kohnstam out in 1958, after complaints about Kohnstam's handling of some export markets, and the name Moko was immediately phased out of all Lesney packaging. Lesney also bought out Fred Bronner's US operations, making it a wholly owned subsidiary of the parent company. Bronner, however, remained in charge of the American subsidiary.

Good times

In 1960 the decision was made to go public, and in the same year Peter Webb was lured away from Lesney's advertising and marketing agents to join the company.

This was a successful time for Lesney: by 1966, it employed 3600 workers and was producing more than 100 million models annually. That same year, Fred Bronner founded an American Collectors' Club which would grow to 50,000 members in just six years.

During 1967 and 1968, the firm had sales of over £28 million with a profit of £5 million that gained Lesney a special mention in the Guinness Book of World Records. Lesney was presented with three Queen's Awards to Industry, and Smith and Odell were awarded the OBE during the 1960s. Some 130 different countries formed markets for the 5.5 million models produced each week.

Hot wheels

The introduction of Hot Wheels spelled trouble for Lesney. Mattel Inc, an American toy producer, introduced the line with a $10 million promotional campaign.

Lesney was lucky in that Mattel couldn't even begin to cope with early demand. But at the same time Hot Wheels production was based in Hong Kong, with much lower manufacturing costs. Therefore, in addition

to coming up with a new design, Lesney had to find a way to make cars more cheaply. They decided to develop more automated equipment. Meanwhile, US sales dropped to $6 million from $28 million.

Superfast

Lesney's reaction to the introduction of Mattel's Hot Wheels range was the Superfast series, which became an instant hit. By 1971, most of the line had been converted to Superfast, but the firm still lost money because of startup costs.

Plastic kits came out in 1971. To build the image of its Superfast line-up, Lesney produced the Matchbox Collectors' Club and began financing a professional racing team in Formula Two competition.

BELOW A limited edition framed presentation of the Leyland Titan TD1 bus, including a breakdown of parts, was brought out to advertise Swan Pens.

Cascade, a mechanical game, was created and in 1973, the Rola-matics were introduced. These miniatures had working features that functioned as the car was pushed along. The Fighting Furies – romantic action figures – were announced in 1975.

In 1978, Lesney bought AMT, an American maker of plastic model kits, and the American firm Vogue Dolls. But instead of saving the situation, these acquisitions triggered a downturn from which Lesney would not recover.

The end of Lesney?

Jack Odell, who had retired in 1973, was called out of retirement, but was unable to stem the tide.

In 1980, David CW Yeh of the Universal Group put down Lesney's troubles to high labour costs in the UK and the failure by the company to pay enough attention to the American market.

In June 1982, receivers were appointed and a company called Matchbox Toys was created to serve as a holding company for all former Lesney operations. In September 1982 David Yeh became the head of Universal Matchbox.

By the end of 1987, the manufacture of all Matchbox die-cast vehicles had been moved to Macau or the People's Republic of China. In the same year, Universal Matchbox bought the Dinky trademark and made plans to expand its die-cast vehicle range.

On 13 July 1992 Tyco Toys Inc, an American toy company and the fourth largest of the world's toymakers, announced that it had agreed to purchase Universal Matchbox Group Ltd for $106 million.

The future

Not much is known about the future for Matchbox under Tyco, but before acquiring Matchbox, Tyco's sales were concentrated in the US with only 14 per cent overseas. What Tyco has bought with Universal Matchbox is a strong international sales network. Most important, the future of Matchbox as part of the Tyco empire, with sales of over $715 million, is assured.

But the Lesney story doesn't end there. Jack Odell decided in 1982 to begin a new company to produce a line of die-cast toys within the UK. The Models of Yesteryear had been his first love, and he decided to have his new company – Lledo – make a similar line.

CHAPTER ONE

HOW THEY WERE MADE

• • • •

Ferraris, Jaguars, Mercedes Benzes and BMWs are expensive cars requiring wealthy buyers. But adding the latest models of these vehicles to the Matchbox die-cast range represents even more of an investment than simply buying a full-sized vehicle from a car showroom.

Expenses for new-model development run to millions of pounds or dollars, so great care must be taken when selecting new vehicles for future Matchbox toys. The potential popularity of the toy must be weighed against the considerable costs involved in taking it from the drawing board to the end of the assembly line – a process that takes nearly a year.

A new model

So how is a vehicle chosen for a Matchbox run? The research and design department scans car magazines and visits car shows to see the latest vehicles. The Matchbox marketing directors of the United Kingdom, Germany, the United States and Australia then consider the suggestions. Collectors and members of the public also send suggestions to the company. Each marketing manager generally requests four or five models be made for his division, but the total of new miniatures a year is around ten, so compromise is necessary.

ABOVE AND BELOW The Porsche 944 Turbo has opening doors, the Mercedes 500 SL authentic rubber tyres.

Rather than run-of-the-mill cars, the company has been more interested in selecting cars known the world over, such as BMWs and Ferraris. They have also selected cars that capture the imagination, like the super-fast Jaguar XJ220.

Final decisions generally favour the desires of managers from the countries with the highest Matchbox die-cast sales. Recently, the United Kingdom and Germany have had the most clout, while the United States has had to take something of a back seat with only about 25 per cent of sales.

Research

Once compromises are made and new models are chosen, the research and design department goes to work. The real vehicle must be found, either in the form

of a model or as the real thing in a car showroom. It then takes two men about a day to photograph the details of the car from every angle.

Next, a rough sketch of the car itself is made for logging measurements, because even the drawings of a car provided by the manufacturer are not sufficiently accurate for making a model. With this information a draughtsman can then make additional, very detailed, drawings at three times the size of the toy. This process will usually take three weeks.

Completed copies of their drawings are taken to two types of model makers — one who will machine and carve a model out of solid Perspex in the actual size of the toy and another who will make a wooden master model at three times the size of the final toy. The Perspex model is often shown in the catalogue.

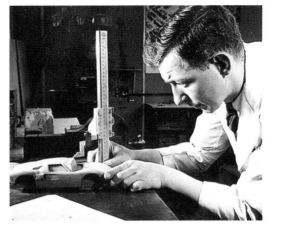

How models were made

In the days when the models were still being made in Britain, moulds carved from chrome-vanadium steel, were put into an automatic die-casting machine from which over one million models were cast. The rough castings were then tumbled and deburred, removing any excess metal to create a smooth surface. Next, all grease, acid and dirt was removed, so that the models could be painted.

Each day more than 2000 gallons of lead-free paint were then sprayed onto the castings, while the paint shop applied colourful finishes to more than 8 million parts. The plastic shop used 60 large plastic moulding

FAR LEFT The machines producing die-castings for models numbered 130. Each machine could produce more than 10,000 cars a day.

LEFT Caravan trailer bodies are spray-painted as they travel towards the oven. The machine can paint thousands of models per hour.

Up-to-date methods

In more recent days, however, copies of the draughtsmen's drawings, photographs, master patterns and the Perspex models have been forwarded to the Hong Kong headquarters of Universal Matchbox before being sent to various production facilities in the Far East.

Resin castings are now made of component parts of the model, three times the completed vehicle size. They are then copied down to the size of the model on machines called 'pantographs'. These cut the delicate outline of a new Matchbox series model in high quality chrome steel. The steel portion of the mould is then hand-fitted and rough castings are taken to check that the mould-making has been accurate. Finally, tool makers check details on high speed die-cast moulds.

ABOVE AND RIGHT The final assembly of the components was done by hand. Even transfers were applied by hand before tampo printing.

machines in order to produce miniature wheels, seats, tyres and other parts. Once the metal and plastic parts were ready, they were put together on 20 different assembly lines. On each side of the assembly lines, technicians used automatic machines to install windows and other plastic parts and to fasten the models to the base plates.

Once they were fully assembled, the new models were inserted into boxes and shipped around the world.

COLLECTING

• • • •

More people collect die-cast toys, and Matchbox in particular, than any, other type of toy. One of the reasons for this is the relatively reasonable prices still charged. Recent miniatures can usually be purchased for well under £1.25 ($2).and even older Matchbox collectables are still affordable. Very few pieces would be valued at more than £62.50 ($100); even fewer command more than £625 ($1000). So while the collector is generally not going to get fantastically rich collecting Matchbox toys, neither will he or she become bankrupt buying the collection.

It is probably a good thing that not all collectors in a particular country are attracted to collecting the same items. For example, the two sides of the Atlantic view things quite differently. In the United States there are many collectors who specialize in the entire 1–7.5 series from early Lesney, days through the Superfast changeover and on to the Universal years. However, in the UK and most of Europe, the 1–75 series, post-Superfast models in particular, are usually viewed as toys, and those who do collect the 1–75 series collect the older, regular-wheeled versions. The most popular series to collect in the UK and Europe is the Models of Yesteryear range.

In his book *Collector's Guide to Toys, Games & Puzzles,* Harry Rinker explains what he calls the 'thirty year rule'. This rule states that for the first thirty years in the existence of any object, its value is purely speculative. In order for the object to increase in value, three things have to happen – which takes thirty years. First, people

LEFT An actual model (in the box) and preproduction model of the Model A Ford Van.

broken or become worn, leaving the collector with a rare, mint-condition collectable. On the other hand, models that immediately found their way onto collectors' display shelves –such as Models of Yesteryear – are more likely to survive, meaning that their price is less likely to climb.

Where to start

It is essential to start with a plan for collecting. It is then a good idea to choose, and stick to, one particular line.

Most long-term collectors agree that the best place to start a collection is with the current models within the line that you have chosen and then to keep up with new issues as they become available. With your collection under way, you might then want to start looking for

must have time to throw things away, thereby reducing the number of copies of the item. Second, an item must be sold and resold, to establish its value. Finally, there must be time for people to become sentimental about objects from their childhood. In addition, with advancing age comes the prosperity necessary to afford luxuries. It is not difficult to see why collecting Matchbox is increasing in popularity.

New collectors

When starting up there are a number of things that any new Matchbox collector should bear in mind. First, a collector must decide what line he or she is going to collect – the 1–75 line, Models of Yesteryear or even catalogues.

Remember that those items that are played with as toys, such as the 1–75 range, are most likely to be

previous models in that line. However, do remember that increasing age and scarcity mean price increases, so start filling in the gaps in your line from previous models as soon as you can afford to.

Essentially, the market for any collectable is controlled by the number of that item that was made. Matchbox and Lledo, like most companies, guard their production figures fiercely, keeping the collector at a disadvantage. There may be speculation, and even leaks from insiders, but the vast majority of these statistics are never known for sure. Be wary of production figures and promises of limited editions. If a model is especially popular, the company will always be tempted to bring out more models. While a catalogue might list a number produced, that number could be wrong even before the number is published. At one point a book quoted a figure of 5000 for a specific Lledo model. Jack Odell decided to check the figure, and found that the number produced was in fact closer to 25,000.

Throughout the world of collecting there is usually someone hoarding items through which he or she hopes to control the market by careful release. These 'suppliers' wield great power and many collectors discover that dealing with such people becomes almost a necessity because they have what no one else does.

Of course, a sudden huge release onto the market of a particular product would lower the value of everyone's collection, including the person who had released it, so it is in the best interests of these collectors to act responsibly.

ABOVE Although it is still quite easy to find K–16 articulated tankers with Texaco, Shell or Aral liveries, this Quaker State version is particularly rare.

COLOUR VARIATIONS

Beware the effects of the sun. The Y5–1 Bentley on the right started life the same colour as its sister (below left), but exposure to ultraviolet rays turned it to the blue colour you can see here.

Although normally found with bright red seats, some of the Y10–2 Mercedes were made with black seats.

Small differences in a model are a source of great interest to collectors. This Y10–1 Mercedes nearly always comes in a light cream colour, but some rare examples are pure white.

RIGHT This Y5–1 Bentley has changed from its original green to blue as a result of exposure to the sun.

BELOW AND LEFT This Y10–1 Mercedes is usually found in a light cream colour (left). The pure white example (below) is therefore rare and of great interest to collectors.

ABOVE This model shows the original green colour of the Y5–1 Bentley — unharmed by ultraviolet rays.

If you are serious about collecting, and especially if you have your eye on the older models, you will eventually need to seek out these 'suppliers'. In the end, they are the ones who will be able to supply virtually all that you require for your collection, and surprisingly, they may even charge somewhat lower prices than those of the smaller collectors.

Books for collectors

As a collector, knowledge of your subject is essential. Too little knowledge can mean a collection that costs too much and is worth too little. A good place to start building your knowledge is with the books on the subject. The major titles available are described overleaf.

LEFT This Highway Express set, in its original box, includes a Supergas petrol tanker, a Uniroyal tractor trailer and a lorry with trailer and speed boat.

A helpful book for the first-time collector of toys is Harry Rinker's *Collector's Guide to Toys, Games & Puzzles* (Radnor, Pa: Wallace-Homestead Book Company, 1991).

The largest and most comprehensive book on Matchbox was issued as part of its 40th anniversary. *Collecting Matchbox Toys – The First Forty Years* is by Kevin McGimpsey and Stewart Orr (Chester, England: Major Productions, 1989) and is available directly from Matchbox and from some dealers.

Charlie Mack has produced a number of volumes on the various Matchbox ranges. *Lesney's Matchbox Toys – Regular Wheel Years 1947–1969* (West Chester, Pa: Schiffer Publishing, 1992) takes a full-colour look at the early Matchbox toys and contains a price guide.

Mack has also written *Matchbox Models of Yesteryear* (Durham, Ct: Matchbox USA, 1989), and two more books – one covering the Superfast years (1969–82) and another chronicling the Universal years (1982–92).

Dr Edward Force penned *Matchbox and Lledo Toys,* a combination of an older Matchbox-Lledo price guide and variations list. Mostly in full colour, it covers modern Matchbox production of the 1–75 series, Dinky,

Superfast Specials, Twin Packs, Models of Yesteryear, Convoy, SuperKings and some other special lines.

The Matchbox Toy Price Guide (3rd Edition) (London: AC Black, 1990) was written by Frank Thompson. This detailed, complete price guide book covers the entire production of Matchbox toys, souvenir items and catalogues, from 1953 until 1990. It is a wealth of detailed information about the various models arranged by type and number.

Paul Carr has produced a book *Collecting MB38 Model A Ford Vans,* copies of which are available by writing to Carr at Unit D–10, The Seedbed Centre, Langston Road, Loughton, Essex IGIO 3TQ, UK.

Philip Bowdidge has published a number of booklets about Matchbox collecting, mostly concentrating on the UK market. His works deal mostly with the 1–75 range, the Major Packs, and the Accessory Packs. Bowdidge is one of the few sources of information about the Matchbox boxes in which various lines were packed. Some collectors claim to be collecting just the boxes, but it is more likely that they are really serving as sources of boxes for those collectors who

need the original box to complete a certain model. Bowdidge has also produced a booklet on the Matchbox catalogues between 1957–1990. His works can be secured by writing to Mr Bowdidge at 8 Melrose Court, Ashley, New Milton, Hants, BH25 5BY, UK.

Specifically for catalogues, an American collector, Lt Col James W Smith, 431 George Cross Drive, Norman, Ok 73069 USA has produced a photocopied listing showing pictures of all of the catalogues that have been issued, descriptions of their differences, and summaries of those published in languages other than English.

Prices

Many of these books contain price guides to help the collector with the valuation of models. Although no collector really likes them, price guides are grudgingly seen as necessities. By the time price guides are written and printed, they are mostly out of date. Also

LEFT The Mod Rod No 1 in some of its various guises. Differences include variations in body, wheel and engine colour.

27

WHITE ROSE

White Rose Collectables of York, Pa (Pennsylvania) was founded in 1989, and the company's growing line of products, which are made by Matchbox, accounted for fully one-third of all Matchbox sales in the United States during 1992.

A new company

Ron Slyder founded White Rose along with his partner Chris Huber after being inspired when he was passed by a NASCAR Transporter on the motorway. As a Matchbox collector for nearly 20 years and proprietor of a shop that specialized in old and new Matchbox Toys, Slyder had a good idea of what sold and what didn't. He could immediately see the appeal of these transporters to Matchbox collectors, racing fans and racing collectors alike.

Slyder discussed his plan with a longtime friend, Chris Huber, and the pair took action. They named their company 'White Rose' taken from the nickname of the Pennsylvanian city in which they were establishing their company. Their products would appeal to collectors, rather than to toy buyers, hence the addition of 'collectables' to the company name.

They first had to find out whether Matchbox would make the models for them. The company agreed to do so, but the pair realized they would need to work out licensing agreements with the NASCAR teams. Their first stop was the Hardee's Racing Shop where they met with Cale Yarborough and his team manager, Bob Tomlinson. Then they went onto Sports Image and Hendrick's Motorsports before they finally met up with Richard Petty. Yarborough showed them how a NASCAR team runs and the White Rose founders were given his permission to do a Hardee's transporter. Richard Petty gave them the go-ahead to include the racing team in their plans.

That first year, they managed to produce four Superstar Transporters: the Dale Earnhardt Goodwrench Racing Team Transporter; the Richard Petty STP Racing Transporter; Cale Yarborough's Hardee's Racing Transporter and the Neil Bonnett Cilgo Racing Transporter.

New lines

The NASCAR vehicles are White Rose's best-known products, but among other products in its line have been two years' of Matchbox MB38 Model A Ford vans bearing baseball and football team logos. Now, however, Slyder and Huber have switched from the MB38 to a 1939 Chevy panel truck (M8245) for their most recent line of football team vehicles and Corvettes for the baseball team vehicles. Nevertheless, the original Superstar Transporter Series remains the company's most popular line. White Rose sales really got under way for the newest additional series

transporters. Two were launched, the company's first three-piece Convoy and the first single Lumina car, both carrying the Goodwrench racing team logos.

White Rose's strategy of producing top-quality, limited-production models has been seen to work and is evidence that Americans will buy die-cast models if they are specifically made for the American market.

ABOVE An MB38 (top left) and Chevy Panel Van (top right) carry the Eagles logo. An MB38 (above left) and Chevrolet Corvette support the Phillies.

Imperfections

Imperfections in painting and transfer work make a model unacceptable to one collector and yet more desirable to another. For example, a transfer or decal can be placed upside down on a vehicle. In fact, this occurrence was fairly common, as authorized outworkers, sometimes non-English speaking, were hired to do specialized painting and transfer work. Lesney then had a difficult time making sure that all of the models were identical when issued.

The Matchbox market

In order to get to know the Matchbox market, a new collector should first join a few clubs and organizations. He or she should then start travelling to toy shows, swap meets, meetings of collectors' clubs, club conventions, Matchbox museums and toy shops. Only by doing these things, can a full understanding of the market be gained.

Codes

The code system for classifying Matchbox and Lledo models was created by Ray Bush in response to the problem of models being altered to look like rare ones. It is based on three categories – Codes 1, 2 and 3 – that are used to identify real and ersatz Matchbox models.

ABOVE AND BELOW The 1969 catalogue introduced movable front wheels. The tractor transporter (below) had a mechanical winch.

price guides sometimes try to set prices, rather than reflect them. If a price given in a guide is high, market prices can rise to meet it. On the other hand, if a price in a guide is much lower than the current price on the market, it could actually drive the market price down.

Fakes

Fraudulent models can be a problem for any Matchbox collector because Matchbox production is and was so assorted that it would be very difficult for any collectors' guide to show or list all the variations produced either by Lesney or by Universal Matchbox. . Obviously, with Matchbox activities in over 144 countries and actual production going on in some of those, creating any guide that would (or could!) list all of them is nearly impossible.

In one particularly notorious scam, unscrupulous dealers took Lledo's first DG–5 model, a horse-drawn fire engine which was selling at the time for about £2, and filed off the Lledo name from the base and repainted it red. It was then sold as the original Lesney Models of Yesteryear horse-drawn fire engine which, at the time, was selling for about £175. A truly knowledgable collector would have known that the Days Gone series from Lledo is slightly smaller than the Lesney Yesteryear series.

BELOW This fake Y12–3 was made in Poland in about 1984. Made of plastic it is unlikely to fool any knowledgable collector who sees it close up.

A Code 1 vehicle is one that was completely produced by Lesney or its successor. That includes all labels, decals or tampo printing. Code 2 is one that was altered by a third party but with the complete written approval of the Lesney or Matchbox management. Code 3 is a normal Lesney or Matchbox model that was changed in colour, design, or decoration without the knowledge or approval of Lesney or Matchbox.

MICA

When the UK Matchbox Club folded in 1985, the Matchbox International Collectors' Association (MICA) took its place. MICA produces six magazines per year, with articles on Yesteryear models; early, rare regular wheel and Superfast models; and catalogues; readers' news and views; listings of upcoming collectors' fairs, news from the Australian and USA Matchbox markets; and a classified advertisement section. The Association also holds annual conventions. New members are welcome. Send a stamped, addressed envelope or two International Reply Coupons to your local club representative.

USA and Canada The Membership Secretary, MICA North America, 585 Highpoint Avenue, Waterloo, Ontario, Canada N2L 4Z3.

UK and Europe The Membership Secretary, MICA; 13 Lower Bridge Street, Chester CH1 1RS, UK.

Australia and New Zealand MICA Coordinator; Matchbox Toys Pty Ltd, 5 Leeds Street, Rhodes. Sydney, NSW 2138, Australia.

Matchbox in the USA

The Matchbox USA club offers monthly magazines concentrating mainly on the miniatures and Yesteryear ranges, and containing a classified section. Write to Matchbox USA, Rural Route 3, Box 216, Saw Mill Road, Durham, Connecticut 06422, USA. Enclose a stamped, addressed envelope or two International Reply Coupons.

Charles Mack, head of Matchbox USA, also oversees the Matchbox Collectors' Club that produces a quarterly newsletter. For information, write to Charles Mack at PO Box 278, Durham, Ct 06422, USA.

One of the few surviving small clubs is the Pennsylvania 'Matchbox' Collectors' Club. It publishes the Pennsylvania Matchbox

Newsletter, which provides limited information about new releases and the collecting of Lledo models. Membership can be obtained by writing to William J. Charles, 2015 Old Philadelphia Pike, Lancaster, Pa 17602, USA.

American International Matchbox Inc (AIM) was founded in May 1970 by Harold Colpitts of Lynn, Massachusetts. For membership details, write to American International Matchbox Inc, 532 Chestnut St, Lynn, Ma 01904, USA.

Lledo collectors

For Lledo collectors, there is a magazine, Lledo Calling, and an international Lledo club. There are five newsletters a year providing information about Days Gone, promotional models and souvenir models. *The Days Gone Collector* contains information about the Days Gone models. For information about either or to subscribe write to the New Subscriptions Department, PO Box 1946, Halesowen, West.

CHAPTER THREE

POPULAR
COLLECTABLES

• • • •

While any of the Matchbox ranges offer the first-time collector enough options to begin his or her journey through the world of Matchbox, there are certain popular models of Matchbox production, both current and past, which consistently find their way into the major collections.

There even seem to be national preferences, with collectors in one country seeking out models avoided by most collectors from other countries. This obviously affects the prices that these models command in their respective countries.

Early toys

Prior to 1953 and the introduction of the first die-cast miniature, Lesney toys were generally not packaged in individual boxes. Instead they were shipped in large boxes containing a dozen of each toy in a rainbow of colours. The individual boxing of the models began officially in 1949 with the production of the Horse-drawn Milk Cart, sometimes referred to as a 'float'.

Produced during this period, from 1948 to 1955, were the Aveling Barford Road Roller, Cement Mixer, Crawler Tractor (sometimes called a Caterpillar Tractor), Crawler Bulldozer (Caterpillar Bulldozer), the

BELOW The rear tyres on this tractor were put on backwards – so the tread went the wrong way.

A number of the early toys were marketed with accessories. The Milk Cart came with a driver and six metal milk crates filled with bottles; the Rag-and-bone Cart came with a similar driver and an assortment of die-cast junk to add realism.

Colours varied, because as Jack Odell pointed out, in the years after the War, and even into the early 1950s virtually everything was rationed and shortages in industrial materials were particularly bad.

Some rare specimens include any model of the Rag-and-bone Cart (green ones are especially rare), the Soapbox Racer and blue milk floats.

Horse-drawn Milk Cart, the Rag-and-bone Cart, the Soapbox Racer, Jumbo the Elephant, the Prime Mover, Trailer and Bulldozer, Muffin the Mule, Large Coronation Coach, Small Coronation Coach, Massey Harris Tractor, the Bread Bait Press, and a Covered Wagon.

ABOVE AND BELOW Only ten Soap Box Racers (above) are known to exist. The covered wagon (below) was the last of the early Lesney toys.

Several models that were conceived but never released as full-size Lesney models later formed the bases for some of the early miniatures or Yesteryear models.

Regular wheels

The 1–75 series of Matchbox toys came into existence in 1953 and remains probably the most accessible to

collectors on both sides of the Atlantic. The first three to roll off the production line were, No 1, the Aveling Barford Road Roller, No 2, the Muir Hill Site Dumper, and No 3, the Cement Mixer. Over the years, the make-up of the range has changed. According to the success or otherwise of the models, some issues have been discontinued due to a drop in sales and others have been reissued with new bodywork. But the number in the range has not exceeded 75 since 1980.

Within the regular wheels series, a number of noteworthy vehicles exist. The MG Midget TD (19A) in 1956 became the first passenger car created for the series. Its warm reception assured collectors of Matchbox miniatures that Lesney would continue to keep new car issues rolling.

The first American vehicle was steered into the Lesney miniature line in 1957. The 31A (or 31–1), Ford Customline, sold very well. Not long afterwards, in 1959, an American Ford Thunderbird (75A) was the first car to have plastic windows from the start.

The American Ford Thunderbird was also a milestone in that the series had arrived at the number 75. Actually, there had been no firm plans to stop the series at 75, but

ABOVE The small coronation coach was produced in 1953. It came with eight horses and was available in gold or silver.

RIGHT The Massey Harris Tractor miniature No 4 had rotating wheels, but the ivory-coloured driver could not be moved from his seat.

MB38s

ABOVE This MB38 promoted Matchbox and was available at the 1984 New York Toy Fair (as displayed on the roof of the vehicle).

The Model A Ford Van (38G) has a special place in the history of Matchbox. It has been marketed not only as a regular issue in the 1–75 line of miniatures but also as a promotional model and is therefore to be found in hundreds of different versions, with dozens of advertising or special occasion messages and a rainbow of colour combinations for its base, body and roof.

Promotional vehicles

Matchbox itself has used the vehicle for sales and advertising messages, such as a special run of vehicles produced as give-aways for corporate toy buyers who were attending the 1984 New York Toy Fair. This model displayed the message: 'Matchbox on the Move in '84' on its side and 'Toy Fair '84' on its roof.

The company has also made special MB38s for collectors, including the 'Matchbox USA' model for Americans and the all-black 1987 model made for the second Matchbox International Collectors' Association (MICA) convention dinner.

Companies have used them as promotional items for their own customers or, in the case of the very rare Ben Franklin vans, just 1000 were produced for the company's managers. They have also been issued to mark special company milestones like Reckitt & Colman's 75th anniversary celebration for Silvo Silver Polish.

MB38 collectors

The first regular issue MB38 was produced in 1982 for the 1–75 line. This was the Champion Spark Plugs van, with royal blue cab, black base, white roof and chrome bumpers, headlights and grille, along with the company's red and black logo incorporating a sketch of a spark plug.

In February 1984 an offer was printed on boxes of Kellogg's Cornflakes in the United Kingdom. Consumers simply had to send in four proofs of purchase to receive a free MB38 with side panels

ABOVE Two delightful delivery vans advertising Champion Spark Plugs.

advertising the cornflakes. The promotion ran for six months in the United Kingdom, and was repeated in France in 1986 and in Denmark in 1987. During that time some two million vans were sent out. Not surprisingly, the Kellogg's Cornflakes MB38 is the model now most widely available – a normal issue of a promotional model is about 20,000 vehicles.

Issue 20 in March 1987 was another major factor in the MB38 collection. Only 450 of these models were made for the 2nd MICA convention dinner and their attractive appearance and limited availability, made them particularly appealing.

When White Rose Collectables produced a two year series of MB38s containing baseball- and football-team logos as well as the names and colours of ice hockey and college teams, the hobby of collecting these M838s took a new turn.

LEFT Kellogg's Cornflakes played a big part in the popularity of MB38s, by offering their customers a 'free model van' decorated with the Kellogg's livery.

Some feel this series inspired new collectors of the MB38, but others that the number of models in the series put collectors off, afraid they wouldn't be able to keep their collection complete and up-to-date.

BELOW This simple red, white and blue van is valuable because the models were only ever given to the Ben Franklin management.

LEFT Only 450 of this model were ever made – for the second MICA convention. For that reason it is now a rare and thus valuable van

when it arrived, the company decided to scrutinize the range to decide if any models needed replacement. At that time, it was decided that there was too heavy an emphasis on military vehicles and that some other vehicles were losing their appeal. Also, shop owners were beginning to get a bit nervous about the space required to display Matchbox products. Thus, Lesney began withdrawing certain models and replacing them with new ones or with new variants of existing ones.

Wheel colours and materials changed in 1958, with the switch from metal to grey and black plastic wheels.

In 1963, the first model with opening doors, a Mercedes Benz 220 SE coupe (53B), appeared. Next came working suspensions and 'Autosteer' which allowed the car to be steered with only 'simple pressure'. In 1969, an Iron Fairy Crane (42C), became the last new model to be made with regular wheels.

It is worth being aware that during Lesney's most successful years, production topped about 5.5 million models per week with over 75 per cent going for export and 60 per cent of that destined for the United States. Therefore when naming

rare models, what is true for one part of the world might not be true for another. Also, what is prized in one country may be common place in another. It is important that the novice collector finds reliable information that pertains specifically to his or her own country before setting off on the hunt.

In 1969 crisis hit Lesney. With the introduction of Mattel's Hot Wheels, Lesney was plunged into a race for survival and so developed the design for their competing Superfast wheels. As soon as possible, they began changing production from the regular wheels to the Superfast variety. Ultimately, all miniature production would be of the new type. That changeover seriously altered collecting on both sides of the Atlantic.

The differences between the two types of wheel were noticeable. The regular wheels rolled on heavy-duty 1.6 mm axles which were lodged in holes in underside projections and then 'mushroomed' over in order to hold the wheels securely to the axles. The new Superfast design relied on much thinner axles that were only 0.6 mm. They had special inserts that were tailor-made to fit the bases of each different model and the wheels were formed from a special plastic that reduced the friction between the axle and the wheels. Not all the old models, however, could be changed over and some continued as they were, even after the major changeover in 1970.

In the UK, collectors essentially took the changeover to indicate that the models were indeed now toys and not for serious collecting. On the other side of the Atlantic, however, Americans greeted Superfast wheels warmly, and the collecting of the miniatures possibly even increased. Therefore, in the UK, a serious collector of miniatures will almost certainly specialize in the pre-Superfast versions, while in the USA, it will more than likely mean that both are collected.

Superfast

It is safe to say that the introduction of the Hot Wheels range by Mattel in 1969 caused Lesney to take increased notice of its American market. Sales of

LEFT A metallic red Aston Martin, as seen here, is more rare and more valuable than its previous incarnation in metallic green.

Matchbox nose-dived from $28 million annually to $6 million. Most of Lesney's production was for export, and the largest single export market was the US – something had to be done.

With the creation of the Superfast series, the focus of the line-up

LEFT The Iron Fairy Crane, No 42, was the last in the line of new models with regular wheels. After this, Superfast was used on all models.

MATCHBOX

CLASSIC SPORTSCARS OF THE THIRTIES

Models of Yesteryear

1936 AUBURN SPEEDSTER

LIMITED EDITION Nº F 4884

1931 STUTZ BEARCAT

1938 MERCEDES 540K

1928 MERCEDES SS

BOOKLET CONTAINING THE COMPLETE HISTORY OF EACH CAR INSIDE

ABOVE This 'Classic Sportscars of the Thirties' set was made in the early 1980s for the Australian market. Only 5,000 were produced.

shifted. Models would change drastically. Some vehicles that were known only in the UK would be dropped in favour of models with names such as the Baja Buggy (13E), the Wildcat Dragster (8F) and the Dodge Charger (52C). Scorpions, introduced in 1971, were electrically driven cars with rechargeable batteries.

Rola-matics were introduced in 1973. These models had altered Superfast wheels that turned gears, which in turn operated various moving parts, such as turrets,

fans, and radar antennae. Chopper motorcycles were also introduced that year.

With the severe economic turmoil Britain experienced during 1973 and 1974, Lesney was forced to take measures that would result in some unusual issues. The coal miners' strike led to the curtailing of electricity, a three-day working week, and shortages of many industrial supplies. Lesney decided to reintroduce some colours that had been unpopular in the past. They also

Because Brazilian law made the importation of completed products very difficult, in 1977 Lesney began producing parts to be assembled into models in Brazil. The venture made little money for Lesney, but the models created (often in unique colour schemes) are now coveted by collectors.

dredged up decals that had languished for years. Six Superfast models were marked with Scorpion labels (a red scorpion resting on a white circle, surrounded by a black border), even though they were not electrically powered. These models are now rare.

Hot Rods were burning out by 1975 and so were the Rola-matics. The excitement that year was for the first tampo printing appearing on a line of miniatures called 'The Streakers'. Tampo is the process of using a rubber pad coated with ink to print directly on the model.

Special models were also issued for Germany and Japan, often using new colours on old vehicles. The earliest Japanese ones, J1 through J9, were dressed up with attractive new boxes, too.

The new decade brought more changes. New models no longer would have 'Superfast' printed on their base plates.

Promotional Vehicles

The Y5–4 1927 Talbot Van changed the Yesteryear line forever, opening up the world of the promotional vehicle. The Y5–4 Talbot Van featured a Lipton's Tea logo and the Royal Crest. The company had written to the Lord Chamberlain's office, asking to use the crest but, when no reply came, they went ahead and 100,000 had been shipped by the time they heard that permission had been denied. As the news spread, collectors scrambled to buy the models. Luckily the Lord Chamberlain's office didn't require a recall, but the crest was deleted from future production.

From this point on, various types of vans from Ford, Crossley, General Motors, Renault, Mack, Walker, and Morris were plastered with just about every conceivable logo. Probably the most coveted is the early production of the Y4–4, a 1930 Duesenberg Model J Town Car, made in 1976.

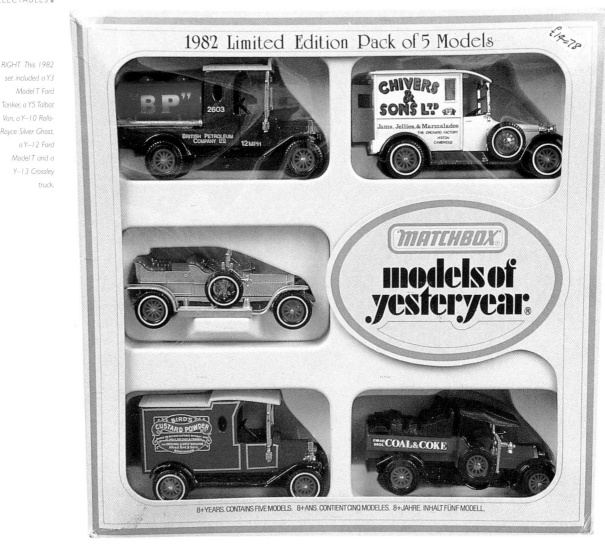

RIGHT This 1982 set included a Y3 Model T Ford Tanker, a Y5 Talbot Van, a Y–10 Rolls-Royce Silver Ghost, a Y–12 Ford Model T and a Y–13 Crossley truck.

More military models were discontinued and toy safety laws were becoming more stringent. A new, stronger design for opening doors was created. The 'Code Red' series of eight models was also produced in line with the new American television programme of the same name.

With the bankruptcy of Lesney and the takeover by Universal, production was shifted to Macau and the line was split into three parts – one for the USA, one for the remainder of the world (ROW) and a CORE line of models used in both groups.

Matchbox would make many special models for everything from the James Bond movie *A View To A Kill* to Chef Boy-ar-dee canned pasta.

Yesteryear

The Yesteryear models are often referred to as Matchbox's 'flagship' range, and this is certainly true as far as the UK and Australia are concerned. Originally, collectors in the UK, France, Germany, and Japan were large buyers of this line, but now Australians are prepared to pay more to buy Models of Yesteryear than Germany and the UK combined.

Because of the numbering changes of the models for various parts of the world, the system was becoming unworkable. A simple solution emerged to stop putting model numbers onto the bases of the 1–75 series. Boxes in which the vehicles were packed were also changed to include a small window. It was a distressing change for collectors because it halted the tradition of the picture box. Dealers liked the idea, however, because it meant being able to do away with cumbersome display shelves.

The year 1984 saw much activity in the models for Australia and Japan. Some recoloured models were issued for the Australian collectors' market and sold as special or limited edition models. Since then, many more such models have been produced. The Japanese line-up of vehicles would climb to 100 models by drawing on issues from other lines and ones painted just for the Japanese market.

In the UK and France, buyers were to be tempted by some Hot-Rod-type American models in boxes festooned with stars and stripes. As time went on,

DISNEY

The Matchbox Disney series, produced by Universal Toys of Hong Kong (before Universal bought Matchbox), is believed to be a fairly safe investment within the world of Matchbox collecting. The line only ran from 1979 until 1980 and was primarily directed at the children's market.

In 1979's pocket catalogue the arrival of these popular characters was announced. Across the tops of pages 36 and 37, the word 'NEW' was used in large letters no fewer than eight times. The product line began with WD–1 (Mickey Mouse piloting a fire engine); WD–2 (Donald Duck driving a beach buggy); WD–3 (Goofy cruising in a Volkswagen Beetle); WD–4 (Minnie Mouse touring in a Lincoln); WD–5 (Mickey in a Jeep); WD–6 (Donald Duck driving a police Jeep).

The catalogue also noted that an additional three models: WD–7 (Pinocchio's Road Show); WD–8 (Jiminy Cricket's Old Timer) and WD–9 (Goofy's Racer), would become available in late 1979.

The 1980/81 catalogue was only slightly less emphatic in its enthusiasm about still more 'NEW' models. An additional three models: WD–10 (Goofy's Train); the WD–11 (Donald Duck driving an ice cream truck) and the

paid for them. Secondly, these models appeal to not only Matchbox collectors but also Disney collectors. The number of potential buyers is thus increased, and with a reduced number of mint models available, this Disney collection becomes all the more desirable and difficult to find.

final models in this batch of Disney products, including the WD–12 (Mickey Mouse driving a Corvette) were introduced at this time.

In the 1981/82 Matchbox catalogue, the company expanded into another Disney character with the Popeye series (copyright King Features Syndicate, Inc). The CS–13 was Popeye's spinach truck. the CS14 Bluto's Road Roller and CS15 Olive Oyl's sports car.

Two aspects of the line have helped to make it particularly appealing to collectors as one to buy and save. First of all, since they were sold as toys, many will have been scratched and damaged, greatly reducing the number of 'mint condition' models available, and therefore, increasing the prices

In Europe, over three-quarters of collectors focus upon the Yesteryear models. US collectors, of whom three-quarters collect the miniature 1–75 series, were probably more influenced by the fact that Fred Bronner, the man responsible for Matchbox's popularity in the USA, did very little to promote Lesney's 'flagship' line.

Collecting Models of Yesteryear has a limited following in the United States, particularly as a result of recent marketing experiments and substantial price increases that have more than doubled the cost of a model. In an attempt to make the model line more popular Matchbox tried direct marketing – which had worked well in Australia.

BELOW In 1992 the Y–34 1933 Cadilac 452 was released. This model is still in perfect condition and in its original box.

Good or bad policy?

From 1991 the Yesteryear and Dinky lines came under Matchbox's 'Specific Model Issue Policy' which provides that starting in 1990, each model may be recoloured only twice during its life, that any new model created from an existing one will be recoloured only once, and that worldwide production, will be limited.

Matchbox claims that this policy will ensure that these ranges will be more collectable, that values will increase more rapidly, and the reduction in numbers will save the collector from having to spend a fortune. Unfortunately, this reduced volume has resulted in steep price rises.

Yesteryear collections

The Models of Yesteryear series was always supposed to appeal to adult collectors. It was never intended to use a standard scale and models were made to present a pleasing proportion to the eye.

Yesteryears virtually had the market to itself. Dinky and Corgi produced nothing like them. Several times in the line's history however, collectors have made complaints. First when Lesney began using metallic paints and then when they introduced whitewall tyres as standard. Fortunately, these minor problems have been overcome. Far more attention is now paid to authenticity and collectability, and in fact, some of those awkward, misguided touches of years ago are the very things that make the line appeal to collectors.

The Yesteryear product line consists of passenger cars and lorries as well as sports and racing cars, steam driven vehicles and buses and trams. The first model was an NHP Allchin Traction Engine (Y1–1), which was trimmed in gold and copper, with a basic livery of green with red wheels.

The Y9 – Fowler 'Big Lion' Showman's Engine, is considered to be a pinnacle in die-casting and in the Models of Yesteryear series.

Another Showman's Engine, the Y19–2 Fowler B6 made Matchbox history as the most costly Yesteryear model ever made. At £18, it was sold with a guarantee that the model would never again be produced.

The Y23–1 1922 AEC Omnibus issued in 1983, encountered problems because of its advertising. Issued with Schweppes signage, the first red labels were unsatisfactory and new ones were ordered in black. Then Schweppes protested that there was no trademark identification and the printing was not in the company's style. A new design, in yellow and black, was finally produced. In the meantime, the few red label models became increasingly valuable.

The Y16–4 1923 Scania Vabis Post Bus, issued in late 1988 to early 1989, is a curious looking contraption. It has skis mounted under its front wheels and

ABOVE This Dodge Viper was never released in the form seen here. There was disagreement with the manufacturers and the mould was changed.

LEFT Most versions of this Y7–1 Leyland lorry will have grey metal wheels. This model was part of the last production run and has black plastic wheels.

a special device enveloping the rear wheels so that the bus was driven by continuous loop rubber treadband – ideal on Sweden's snow-covered winter roads.

Through the years various models have been added to give the line world-wide appeal. The Y102 1928 Mercedez-Benz 36–220, added to the range in 1963, gave life to the German market. Georges Bieber, Lesney's French importer, begged for a French car in the line and got the Y2–2 1911 Renault two-seater passenger car. America was represented by the Y7–2 Mercer Raceabout Sports Car. Racing cars by Bugatti, Ferrari, and Maserati brought Italy into the Yesteryear family.

The Y13–3 Ford Model T Van, produced to celebrate the establishment of the Bang & Olufsen electronics firm and the Y12 for the Hoover Company (both produced in 1981) are collectors' favourites. The Bang & Olufsen truck was painted white and red, with the company logo in red and the firm's name in black letters.

The Y12s for Hoover were produced inside a special steel cage within the factory, to prevent stealing. Painted in blue with gold lettering, and printed with the Hoover motto, the production figure for official models was 540. An additional 20 were given to members of Lesney management, and one to Her Majesty the Queen.

Dinky

In April 1987, Universal Matchbox bought the Dinky trademark and determined that the Dinky line should be similar to that of the Models of Yesteryear but with a more modern accent. The American models in the Dinky range are the best-selling ones, except for the DY–11 and DY–1113 Tucker Torpedo. Some past and present models include the DY–9B, 1949 Land Rover; the DY–21, 1964 Mini Cooper 'S'; the DY–26, Studebaker Goldenhawk; the DY–25, 1958 Porsche 356A coupe; and the DY–27, 1957 Chevrolet Bel Air.

This line is intended to represent the 'cars that Dad drove when I was young', and has been selling reasonably well. The high cost of the models helps reduce the demand for this quality line of die-cast toys.

CHAPTER FOUR

GIFTS AND ACCESSORIES

• • • •

In the 1960s and 1970s, the creative minds within the company set out to capture the imagination of children offering them more than model vehicles. They began by designing accessories, such as the pack containing three Esso petrol pumps, a service station attendant and a tall Esso sign. There was also a set of road signs indicating hazards, such as a double bend in the road, the roundabout, and a train or level crossing. Soon, there were roadways and petrol stations – and that was only the beginning of the Matchbox efforts to make the company's toys more interesting and exciting for their younger market.

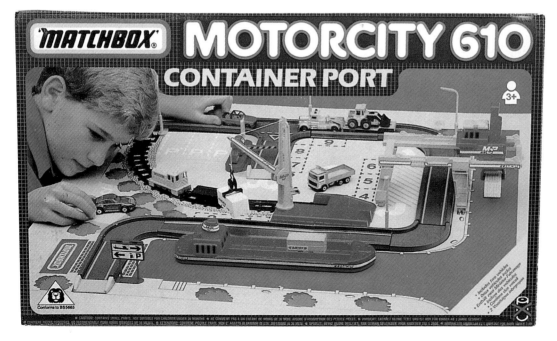

LEFT The Container Port comprised a container ship, crane, railroad track, diesel shunter and roadway playmat.

Matchbox travelling

Roadways were the most obvious accessories for the cars and, through the years, Matchbox designers introduced all kinds of variations that went far beyond the first basic cardboard road mats.

Along with the basic roadway came additional sets like: 'Heart of London', picturing tourist attractions, Big Ben and Tower Bridge, Piccadilly Circus, and well-known streets like Regent Street and Haymarket; 'Queen's London' with Buckingham Palace, St James' Park and Admiralty Arch; and a race track setting, complete with pits and grandstands. Additional sets in this basic cardboard roadway series included the W2 construction site, and the R–3 Farmyard.

After these 'fold away' playgrounds, came the impressive Matchbox 'Build-A-Road', marketed in the United States in the late 1960s. The 1968 pocket catalogue announced this more creative approach to road building: 'Now you can design and build your very own roadway, scaled just right for Matchbox models'. The Super Build-A-Road, with more than 90 pieces and at least seven different possibilities for roadway designs, sold for $7.

Still another option for Matchbox 'drivers' was the Matchbox Motorway that cost a hefty $22.95 in 1969. With special adapters to fit any Matchbox model, variable speed controllers and an electric power pack, cars could race around the track unaided by human hand.

The switch to Superfast wheels ushered in a new era for roadways. Construction sites, farmyards and motorways faded quickly and were replaced by dramatic Superfast Tracks with all kinds of accessories designed to add to the thrills of Matchbox 'driving'. There were, for example, the SF1 Speed Set (a basic drag strip), the SF–2 Loop Set (which took the car in an airborne circle), and the SF–3 Curve and Space Leap Set (after coming around a curve, a car would fly over an open space before landing on more track).

Service stations, fire stations and garages

As well as roadways, Matchbox enthusiasts were tempted with service stations, both one and two storeys high, and a fire station. The BP petrol station had showrooms on two floors and a forecourt for petrol pumps. There was also a service ramp-incline from the ground to the first floor level.

The Matchbox fire station featured side-by-side double doors in the engine house and a firemen's pole from the second to the ground floor. It, like the service station, cost $3 in 1966 and came fully assembled.

Garages have come in all shapes and sizes progressing far beyond the early combination petrol stations and garages. Matchbox Autopark was billed as 'The Sky Park of the Future'. Battery operated, it included a rotating wheel via which

the cars could be parked. The 1972 pocket catalogue featured Matchbox Station Maker which contained all the parts required to build a garage to your own specifications — be they one level or multi-storey.

On the other hand, in the towering three-level Matchbox Super Garage pictured in the 1979/80 and 1981/82 pocket catalogues the features were fixed. On

LEFT The Super Garage had an operating elevator tower for parking cars on the two upper levels and moveable auto ramps. It also had petrol pumps and a rotating sign.

GIFT SETS

It was decided in the late 1970s and early 1980s to market gift sets in a big way. Die-cast vehicles were grouped according to a common theme such as car transporters; railways; racing cars; construction, farm and emergency vehicles; Thunder Jets and Sky Giants. It was a big step from the gift sets of a random combination of vehicles.

The Construction Set G–5 in 1979 included a Load-a-Vator for loading rocks, sand and gravel; a dump truck, a cement mixer, a bulldozer, shovel-nose tractor and a Bomag road roller.

Complete with plastic-fronted accessories made to look like a hospital entrance, the front of a burning building and the front of a police station, the Emergency Set G–7 for 1979 included two types of fire engine (a snorkel fire engine No 13 and a Blaze Buster), an ambulance, a police car and a rescue helicopter and two emergency personnel.

RIGHT A working Load-a-Vator for loading rocks, gravel and sand was the main selling point for this construcion set of five vehicles.

LEFT The emergency vehicles in this set were accompanied by the facades of a hospital, a police station and a burning building.

LEFT In 1972 the Drag Race Set contained six Superfast cars and a Thunderbolt launcher (with extension) to propel them on their way.

the first floor there were car-care, spare parts and service centres and in the rest of the structure an operating parking lift, moveable auto ramps and a rotating Matchbox Garage sign.

Since then, many more freestanding play environments and structures have been produced including construction yards, container ports, lorry parks and even a car wash. All these structures could be called the forerunners to Play Track combinations of roads and buildings, introduced in the early 1980s, and the Motor City sets of the late 1980s and early 1990s.

More than just models

Those collectors interested in other goods relating to the company can search out Matchbox calendars, which were first printed in the 1980s. They can look for an early 1960s series of painting and colouring books. Matchbox picture puzzles, advertised in the 1969 pocket catalogue, featured die-cast models in life-like settings such as a tractor in a field or buses on a mountain roadway. Frames were even made for the puzzles so that they could be hung on the wall once they had been completed.

There was even a Matchbox story book called *Mike and the Model Makers*, a children's version of how Matchbox models were made. It began with Mike's description, 'There was a building so long I could not see the other end. Up on the roof there was a sign. It was a name I didn't know. And in the street, a strange coloured bus for London – blue – then suddenly, another bus came by and I saw on the side of it – 'Matchbox'. Lesney means 'Matchbox'! Now I knew what Daddy meant when he was talking about the greatest automobile factory in the world.'

The Matchbox Traffic Game included two Matchbox cars, mileage measurer, chance cards, game board, traffic signal and instructions. The Matchbox Crash Game, new in 1970, came with four die-cast miniatures. 'Watch your car soar to the front with the throw of a dice – change lanes and outwit your rivals but be careful of the crash area – you can lose your lead'.

Those who remember playing with other Matchbox toys might recall the Magnet Action Centres and the Steer-N-Go toys. The Magnet Action Centres had tiny magnet-operated people who could be moved around to load and service the Matchbox models. There were three different versions available, the Magnetic Action Repair Centre, the Magnetic Action Freight Centre and the Magnetic Action Farm Centre.

Steer-N-Go put young Matchbox fans in the driver's seat. The toy, which included a simulated wood steering wheel, gear lever, ignition switch, hand brake, lap counter and timing device, featured a rotating disc that presented driving challenges similar to those on a real road. There were also three additional driving courses available: the village roadway with six buildings; the dune buggy roadway with marking flags charting a driving course on the sand and a Grand Prix roadway, with a grandstand and finishing gate.

Storage

The customers' need for 'garages' for their cars and lorries brought about another line of products. Matchbox collectors' cases encouraged children to organize and store their die-cast vehicles neatly.

BELOW This carrying case designed to look like a truck was available in two different sizes – to carry either 36 or 48 Matchbox cars.

For those with lots of space, old dealer display cases can be found in cardboard, wood and plastic. They can be filled with vehicles just as they used to be in toy shops everywhere.

Lesney Veteran Car Gifts, produced in the late 1960s and 1970s, marketed the Models of Yesteryear in a new way – with silver and gold finishes and usually mounted on various kinds of giftware. A double pen stand had a 1907 Rolls-Royce Silver Ghost mounted between the two pens. A wooden cigarette box came with a 1911 Model T Ford or a 1928 Mercedes Benz on its lid. Ash trays in the 1967 catalogue were available with any one of six Yesteryear models while pipe smokers had a choice of two vehicles on their pipe trays.

Before the giftware line came to an end, die-cast vehicles would be used on everything from bookends and desk calendars to thermometers and pipe racks.

ABOVE This racing car carrying case was one of the more sophisticated containers dreamt up by the Matchbox designers.

At first, these collectors' cases were basic 'boxes', but later, Matchbox designers came up with some imaginative containers. In 1968 there were two cases, one for 48 models and another for 18, of washable vinyl with nickel-plated locks and plastic handles. A year later there were 72– and 24-model cases with liftout trays. Late came containers shaped like a tool box, a convoy truck, a city garage, a racing car and a steering wheel.

More collectables

Over the years, Matchbox product lines have diversified widely. There have been dolls, plastic models, miniature pub signs, miniature dogs, hand-held plastic puzzles, and even souvenir paperweights featuring such London landmarks as St Paul's and Big Ben.

RIGHT This ashtray, adorned with a beautiful 1934 Riley in silver and red was one in a line of Matchbox souvenirs.

CATALOGUES

• • • •

"MATCHBOX" COLLECTOR'S CATALOGUE | 1965 International Edition

Matchbox catalogues take their readers on a journey through each era's most popular vehicles and provide glimpses of construction, farm and emergency vehicles that helped shape the world.

Using catalogues

It is important to be aware that models shown on the pages of these catalogues were not always what Matchbox finally produced, because catalogue copy needed to be set long before some new models made it to the assembly line. Sometimes, the catalogue sketches or photographs were coloured differently to the final product. Sometimes, the vehicles and playsets didn't make it onto the market until later than promised, if at all. And not everything in every catalogue was available worldwide.

Over the years, catalogues have encouraged collectors to buy Matchbox toys. A few catalogues contained a chart for keeping a running inventory of your collection. Catalogues usually contained a list of new models and repaints as well as the basic listings.

Facts and a quiz

Matchbox catalogues have provided much more than the basic information on buying new vehicles. Early catalogues gave interesting bits of information for enthusiasts – the 1966 catalogue detailed how Matchbox models were made, the 1968 edition how the paper was made for the catalogue itself. Readers were even given inside scoops.

Once there was a quiz to test collectors:

'From which country comes the full-size version of the famous Models of Yesteryear No Y16 Spyker?' (Answer: Holland)

'Why is the prototype of the very famous Models of Yesteryear No Y15 Rolls-Royce called a 'Silver Ghost?' (Answer: The original car was so silent and smooth in its day that the manufacturer christened it the 'Ghost'. The first 'Ghosts' were in a beautiful polished silver finish and soon became known as 'Silver Ghosts'.)

A person who scored nearly 9 out of the 10 correct answers was declared to be a 'Five-Star top-class Matchbox model expert'.

The future

In 1970, catalogue copy writers also speculated about future vehicles and the role Matchbox would play.

They wrote: 'What will cars of the future be like? Obviously low, with aerodynamic styling. Plastic will be used increasingly for body shells. Motorways would have wires beneath their surfaces to instruct the car what to do. Programmed journey cassettes could be slotted into the dashboard, leaving the driver to enjoy the view. Cars could even dispense with wheels altogether and travel on a thin cushion of air, using compressed air for power. In the not too distant future, cars may rely on atomic energy as a source of power. Matchbox, as always, will continue to keep pace with tomorrow – today'.

Superfast

The 1970 issue carried the first notice of the Superfast models. The cover contained the word 'Superfast' surprinted over a rolling wheel, the vehicle illustrations conveyed a feeling of the movement and speed of the new 'Superfast 1–75 series' and the copy was written to tempt the collector.

At the start of the 1–75 catalogue section, writers went even further: 'Think of the fun you will have in matching a Lamborghini Miura against a bus, or a fire engine against a refuse truck. That's racing with a difference – Superfast style'!

Covers and contents

From 1960 to 1963, catalogue covers carried the phrase, 'All the Matchbox pocket-money toys by Lesney' or simply 'Matchbox Series International Pocket Catalogue, Pocket-money toys by Lesney'. But in 1964, the pocket-money phrase was dropped and in its place was the label, 'Matchbox Collector's Catalogue'. In

1976–82, the booklet was called the 'Matchbox Catalogue'. In 1982–83, there was a brief return to 'Collector's Catalogue' before the appearance of the 1983 edition carrying the first of the shortened titles – 'Matchbox 1983' – the style that has continued until the present.

Catalogue covers hint at Matchbox marketing, too. Beginning in 1962, catalogues were printed in other languages for countries where Matchbox had or hoped to have markets. These pocket-sized booklets appeared in French, German, Italian, Spanish, Dutch and Japanese and, sometimes, in other languages.

BELOW This 1970 edition of the US Collector's Catalogue was full of news about the new Superfast series. Even the cover design conveyed speed.

59

Catalogue collectors

Because the catalogues are so much more than mere pages of cars and trucks and other lines of Matchbox products, it's no surprise that they have themselves become collector's items.

Specialized catalogues, like those produced by the Germans or Australians for the Models of Yesteryear, are sought after. The 1976 specialized catalogue of souvenirs is also desirable.

Naturally, the early catalogues and the fold-out sheets are of particular interest. But collecting some of the older catalogues, produced for the European market can be a particular challenge.

Mint, or better-than-mint condition, catalogues command the best prices. To be mint, the booklet should be free of wrinkles, tears, stains or inside markings. They can show a little wear from being touched or passed around a few times. Pristine catalogues are mint-plus – these have never been touched and are found stored in boxes from the printer.

RIGHT The 1967 US catalogue concentrated on the international side of Lesney and explained how models were transported across the world.

ODELL'S LLEDO

● ● ● ●

In 1982, seven years after Jack Odell resigned from Lesney Products, he was asked to return to see if he could save the firm from imminent bankruptcy. Odell commented that taking over Lesney at this time was like being asked to assume command of the Titanic ten minutes before she sank. He would be able to do very little to help.

When the receivers took over, virtually all production stopped because it was not certain whether Lesney's would be bought and by which firm it might be acquired. Jack Odell was particularly worried about the toolroom personnel and tried to think of ways to help them.

When Universal decided to move all Matchbox production out of the UK, meaning the permanent idling of many UK factories, Odell decided to create a line of die-cast toys, larger than the miniature Matchbox series and yet not quite as large as his Yesteryear brainchild. The result was Lledo – the name a throwback to his code name during his army years – his name spelled backwards.

The first six Lledo models were created in the development toolrooms at Lesney. Odell chose the best ten of Lesney's old personnel to be the core of his design and production staff. Even today, most of the machine operators at Lledo are ex-Lesney employees. The first six Lledo models were released at Easter 1983 and numbered 001–006. They included a Tram

BELOW The horse-drawn fire engine DG5 was the fifth in the line of Lledo models.

ABOVE This tram,
pulled by a black
horse, was called
the 'Downtown 3'
and was the first
of several horse-
drawn Lledo
products.

(DG001), a Milk Float (DG002), a Delivery Van (DG003), an Omnibus (DG004) and a Fire Engine (DG005). The final model issued, and the biggest success of the six, was a Ford Model T Van (DG006).

Five of these first six models were less than overwhelming successes. Having a soft spot for horse-drawn vehicles, Odell created far too many of the first Lledo product. Ultimately, Odell had to admit that the mechanically-powered vehicles sold much better and the horse-drawn ones were dropped from the line.

At about this time, the first promotional issues were created, opening up a market that would prove both boon and bane to collectors. The Model T Ford Van, in the style of the Models of Yesteryear became the basis for the promotional models because of the large area on the sides of the vans on which tampo

and labels could be placed. Odell accepted orders for very short run models in different colours and with different logos.

The creation of the promotional models produced a problem in that it was necessary to identify the two lines. Ultimately, the undersides of the cars were marked either 'Days Gone' or 'Promotional Model'.

*RIGHT Model T
Ford Tankers were
also used as
promotional
vehicles – this one
advertises
Marshall's Fuel
Service.*

62

Queries about the promotional model range are fairly common because the earliest production samples did not possess the identifying insert on their undersides. However, most knowledgeable collectors now know those models that were really early promotional models but issued within the Days Gone line. A bigger problem are those Code 3 models that were originally Days Gone samples that have been changed without Lledo approval by unauthorized third parties. (Lledo models also utilize the coding system used for the Matchbox lines.)

Because of the small scale of the venture, Lledo wanted to avoid involvement in warehousing and sales. Odell used a separate marketing company to handle the distribution of Lledo – the Saltern Agency, operated by Andrew, son of Leslie Smith. However, problems developed and ultimately Lledo took over Saltern.

The year 1984 saw the issue of seven new Days Gone models: a Ford 'Woody' Wagon (Estate), DG0071; a Model T Ford Tanker, DG0081; a Model A Ford Car (a touring car with no top) DG009; an Albion Single Decker Coach, DG010; a Large Horse-drawn Van, DG011; a Fire Engine, DG012; and a Model A Ford Van, DG013.

Six new models greeted 1985: a Ford Model A Car (with top up), DG014; an AEC Double Deck Bus, DG015. a Heavy Goods Van, DG016: a Long Distance Coach, DG017; a Packard Van, DG018 (first released as an ambulance) and a Rolls-Royce Phantom 11, DG019.

With the introduction of the bus, Lledo discontinued the practice of including a set of plastic figures with each model.

Three more models followed in 1986. They were: the Model A Ford Stake Truck, DG020; a Chevrolet Van, DG021; and a Packard Town Van, DG022. Originally planned as a 1986 issue, the introduction of a Scenicruiser Bus, DG023, was postponed until early in 1987 because of production difficulties. Two Rolls-Royces – a Playboy Convertible Coupe, DG024 and a Silver Ghost Tourer, DG025 – were issued, along with a Chevrolet Bottle Truck, DG026; a Mack Breakdown Truck, DG027, and a Mack Canvas-Back Truck, DG028.

BELOW Featuring more modern vehicles, the Lledo Marathons was not a successful line. This model promotes the Huddersfield Daily Examiner.

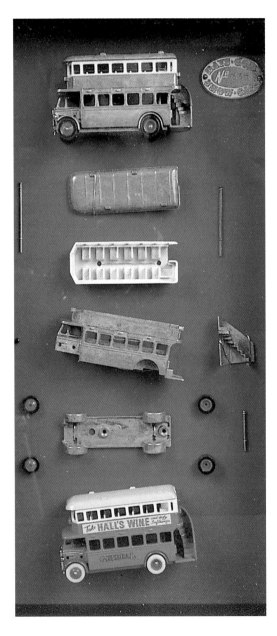

RIGHT The
components of a
DG15 double-
decker bus are
displayed in this
limited edition
presentation case
No 335.

Collecting Lledo

Any collector who decides to collect Lledo will have to make some decisions. First of all, to decide what he or she wants to collect. Of course, there is the regular Days Gone series, including the basic models that were issued in a variety of colours and liveries. There also exists a confusing plethora of promotional models. Lledo has also issued special series of models for various companies, such as Hartoy, Tesco supermarkets in the UK, and the Edocar series in the Netherlands. Lledo has also allowed some of its basic painted production to be altered with scenes from popular UK tourist attractions, thereby creating a number of Code 2 models. In 1987, Lledo issued a new series of models that created a line of modern transportation vehicles in a size slightly larger than the Days Gone line. Called Marathons, these five issues in various liveries were not good sellers and all work on this series has ceased.

What you decide to collect might be affected by availability. In the US, Lledo distribution is patchy at best.

Fakes

The logo of a regular Days Gone model is printed with tampo, but the promotional models also use labels and decals, which is one way for collectors to tell the promotional models from the regular series. However, the Code 3 models also use decals and transfers, and it is sometimes impossible to tell the Lledo issued promotional models from the Code 3 ones.